Please consult a licensed professional before attempting any techniques outlined in this book.

By reading this book, the reader agrees that under no circumstances is the author responsible for any losses, direct or indirect, that are incurred as a result of the use of information contained within this book, including, but not limited to, errors, omissions, or inaccuracies.

How to Start a Moving Company

Discover How to Consistently Land Jobs and Control Your Own Destiny

Kaleb Lambert

Table of Contents

Introduction

Moving. It absolutely sucks. Carrying out big and bulky items, loading them into a truck, taking them out of a truck, and moving them into a new location is no small matter.

However, when something is painful and difficult, there's definitely an opportunity to be had. A typical person simply isn't going to want to deal with the pain and logistics of moving themselves. This is especially the case if they have a lot of things.

This is where you come into the picture. You can solve this issue completely and get paid to do it. Sure, is moving the most glamorous thing this world has to offer?

No, far from it. That doesn't matter though. All that matters is that if you keep it moving, you're getting paid. You can get paid very well in this industry.

Even with that being the case, starting a moving company isn't as simple as getting a box truck and being ready to go. There are a lot of other things you have to think about. What supplies do you need to get started?

How do you establish the business? How can you move customers in a way that's efficient and also protect their belongings from damage? How much should you charge a customer?

How do you even get a customer in the first place? What if you want to grow the business so you can take a backseat and not have to physically be a part of the moving process? Needless to say, there's a lot that goes into starting a moving company.

It can certainly be overwhelming, which is the last thing that you want to feel. Don't worry though, this book will be there for you to help guide you through the process. Certain parts of this book, such as scaling the business, may not be applicable to you right away.

That's okay because it will be there when the time comes for it. Everything will be broken down for you in a way where you can handle things in bite-sized chunks.

There's a lot of work that will have to be done, but that's nothing that people in the moving industry aren't used to. The hard labor will be well worth the pay out. So let's go ahead and get you started on this amazing new journey!

Chapter 1: Reasons Why You Should Get Into the Moving Business

Right now, you might be pondering if starting a moving company is a good idea or not. Maybe you've previously worked for a moving company before. Maybe you already have a box truck and are looking for a way to make good use out of it.

Maybe you want to start a business and just aren't quite sure what kind of business you should start. No matter what phase of life you're in, I want to share with you some reasons why this business is a good idea. The last thing you want to do when starting a business is to dip your toes in the water.

You shouldn't feel hesitant about starting a business. You shouldn't have doubts about what you're doing or if you'll succeed. You want to have confidence in your chosen field and what you're doing. After reading this chapter, you should have no doubts as to why this is a great business to start.

It's Hard and Strenuous Labor

This is something I briefly talked about in the intro, but why is it a good thing that moving is hard and strenuous? It's because people won't want to do it themselves! You might think that you're going to be without work because moving may be hard, but it can be done by physically able people.

Therefore, you'd think that a moving company would be hurt by people who want to do it themselves. Let me tell you, that simply isn't the case! Consider a few factors. Let's assume we are dealing with someone who's moving and is physically capable of moving normal household items.

There could be certain items that the person simply can't move on their own! If you stick around in the industry long enough, you'll definitely come across some interesting and unique items. You'll also come across some very big and bulky items.

A person may have an item or items that are best moved by a professional team. Even if we're just talking about normal household items such as mattresses, tables, couches, and refrigerators, a normal person will struggle to move these items on their own. They're going to have to enlist the help of friends or family.

As I'm sure you may already know, helping a friend move can be great if they pay you or a real pain if they don't. Someone simply might not have friends that live close by who can lend a helping hand, or they might not be willing to help. Even if the person wants to move on their own, they might have to enlist outside help due to necessity.

Another factor that gets people to call a moving company is if the person is on a time crunch. For instance, they might have a reason that's causing them to be moved as soon as possible. They could complete the move themselves, but it would simply take too long.

A moving company could come in and complete the job in a much faster timeframe so the customer will avoid doing the move on their own. All-in-all though, most people will call you up simply because they don't want to deal with the hassle of moving everything themselves. A moving company really does make everything nice, simple, and easy.

Most people simply don't own even a regular pick-up truck. However, with a normal pick-up truck, you're going to have to make multiple trips to complete the job. This is where a box truck would be used instead, which most people definitely don't have.

The individual would still have to rent the box truck, coordinate with someone else to help them pick it up, load everything, drive to the new spot, unload everything, and then drop off the rental. That's exhausting, but some people do that. Compare that to hiring a moving company; the customer makes one call and everything is taken care of.

It's thanks to this ease that people will pay good money for you to get the job done. Additionally, some people simply might not be physically able to execute a move. They're going to have to get outside help either from friends and family or a moving company.

Most people simply won't want to burden their friends and family with a move, so they'll call a company. Ultimately, there's always going to be demand for moving companies for one reason or another!

Great for Physical Activity

The thing with being a mover is that you'll easily accumulate 15-20,000 or more steps per day with ease. You don't even have to think about it.

In a world where heart disease and other such health related issues are on the rise, this is a really good thing.

A lot of people in the modern era work a desk job, which is totally fine. The downside to a desk job is that it can be hard to get in physical activity. You have to go out of your way and really try in order to achieve 10,000 steps per day.

That's never going to be the case when you're working as a mover. Sure, moving may not be looked at as the most glamorous job, but who cares? What matters is that you're getting paid, and you're getting paid to keep your body moving; this is a win win in my book.

People Are Always on the Move

For one reason or another, people are always on the move. People get new jobs that require them to relocate. People want to retire in a different place, so they move.

People move to save money. People are tired of living in the city, so they move to a more rural area or vice versa. People move to go off to college.

People move because their lease is ending. They might need more space or their rent increased by too much and they need to find a different place. Relationships form and people move in together.

Breakups happen, and people move out. There's a whole list of reasons that I could go on and on about. At the end of the first point, I mentioned how there will always be demand for this business, and these are some of the many reasons why!

Chapter 2: What Do You Need to Do to Get Everything Up and Running?

In this chapter, I want to give you everything you need to know to get this business started. I will describe the various supplies you'll need and some of the things you're going to need to do in order to properly set up and establish your business. This is going to be a pretty beefy chapter, so let's not waste any more time.

What Supplies Will You Need?

When it comes to starting a moving company, there's always going to be some different supplies that you will need. The start-up costs for this business can be quite hefty if you don't have anything to begin with. If you just so happen to already own a box truck, then consider yourself lucky because that will be your single biggest initial expense. Here are the things you'll need in order to get started:

Box Truck

Starting a moving company without a box truck simply isn't practical. You need to have a box truck to move people from one place to another. Trying to get the job done with a regular pick-up truck isn't going to be the best look, and it's simply going to take you way too much time.

No doubt about it though, box trucks can be expensive. They also come in various sizes such as 16, 20, 24, and 26 feet. Let's say you wanted to get a 16 foot box truck. In the current car market as of the writing of the book, you could still pay $30-40K for a used one with a decent amount of miles on it. This leads me to my first point...

Buy, Lease, or Rent?

When it comes to getting your first box truck, you have a few options. You can buy (and even within buying, you can buy new or used), you can lease, or you can even rent. So what should you do when you're first getting started?

I actually recommend that you start off with renting a truck as you need it. This is, of course, assuming that you don't have a box truck to begin with. The reason why you should rent is because you don't know how busy you're going to be in the beginning.

You might struggle to land jobs consistently, but you're still going to have to make that truck payment each and every month. There's also the issue of not knowing what size to buy. You could just get a 26 foot box truck right from the jump, but that's going to cost more than a smaller size, and what if it's overkill?

Renting trucks allows you to rent the size you need for the job. It can also help give you a good gauge as to what size you'll need to ultimately make a purchase on. Truthfully though, the best reason to do it is to save money.

What if you're only able to get jobs 1 or 2 days of the week when you first start out? If you lease or buy, you're still paying for the truck every day that you have it. Why not just pay for the days when you actually need it?

Yes, it might be a pain having to coordinate a pick up and drop off of the box truck, but I believe it's the smartest way to get started, especially if you don't have the kind of startup capital that you'd like to have. At what point in your business should you consider taking the plunge and buying or leasing your first box truck? You'll know you've reached a certain point when you consistently have jobs.

If you're booking jobs more days of the week than not, it's time to start researching to get your first box truck. So should you lease or buy? If you buy, then should you buy new or used?

Well when it comes to buying or leasing, there are pros and cons of each. When it comes to leasing, you don't have to worry about covering any maintenance that the truck is going to need over time. This can definitely be a big worry off of your plate especially when you're starting out.

However, every time you make a payment, it's as if it's going into thin air. You're not putting that money towards anything. Leasing a box truck isn't exactly cheap either.

I'm not saying that you should completely disregard this option, but you'll likely be better off looking to buy a box truck. With buying a box truck, you can go the new or used route. Yes, it will be costly as you could expect to pay over $100K for a brand new 26 foot box truck, but at least every time you make a payment, you're one step closer to being done with those payments for good.

So should you buy new or used? Well, that's really going to come down to you and what you can afford. Buying new is obviously going to be the better route if you can afford to do so.

Less miles on a box truck is a good thing, and you'll be able to get a warranty on it in case anything goes wrong. However, the downside is the cost. You're definitely going to be paying quite a bit more to buy a new box truck, and you simply might not be able to afford it.

This is why buying a used box truck can be a great option to save you money and still allow you to get the job done. At the end of the day, it's a box truck. There's nothing fancy about it.

It has a big open space in the back, and as long as it gets from place to place, who cares if it looks shiny and new? After enough time on the road and moving items in and out of it, it's not going to look new anyways. So what should you look for when it comes to buying a used box truck?

The first thing is going to be the mileage. If a box truck is well maintained, you could push it up to 300,000 miles or possibly more depending on the size, engine, and if it's heavy or medium duty. However, for the purposes of a moving company, buying a medium duty truck with a diesel engine is going to be the best bet.

You'll also want to get a box truck with a liftgate on it as this will make it far easier to get super big and bulky items in and out of the truck. The same thing goes for getting a ramp. If your truck doesn't come with one, you'll definitely want to invest in a ramp as it will make loading and unloading easier.

It's not going to be uncommon to see used box trucks that already have 100,000 plus miles on them, so don't be surprised by that. If you keep the truck well maintained, you can still get a lot of life out of it, and it can help you save money. The key is that before you purchase the truck, you'll definitely want to get it inspected by a third party mechanic.

You have no idea how previous owners took care of the truck. This is a big decision, and repairs in the beginning are going to be a costly expense that you'll want to avoid. If everything checks out, you can go ahead and take the plunge with a lot more confidence.

What Size Box Truck Should You Buy?

Like I mentioned earlier, box trucks come in various sizes, so what size should you get when it comes to your moving company? Well, moves are going to occur in various sizes. One day you could be moving a one-bedroom apartment and the next you could be moving a mansion.

Don't let this type of variance scare you. The reason for this is because you get to set the pace. As long as the customer has realistic expectations for when the move should be completed, everything will be good.

For instance, you may want to go all out and get a 26-foot box truck to allow you to complete any sized job in the fastest amount of time possible. However, you might be concerned about being able to afford a 26-foot box truck as opposed to a smaller size. If price is what's holding you back, don't be afraid to go with a smaller size.

If you take my earlier advice, you should start off with renting. This will give you different gauges to see how big the move is and how many trips you have to take with a certain sized box truck. What you'll likely find is that you might have to make an extra trip if the person is moving a large home and you have a smaller truck as opposed to a larger truck.

I say, "so what?" If you come across a big move and suspect it taking an extra trip, factor that into your time estimation and communicate how long it will take to the customer. They won't know any different. You don't need to say, "Okay sir, because I only have a 20–foot box truck and not a 24-foot box truck, I'm probably going to have to make an extra trip making it take longer, so I hope you're okay with that?"

If you estimate the move to take 6 hours, then say that along with what can cause the move to take a longer or shorter time (I'll expand on this later), and leave it at that! Seriously, when you're communicating with a customer, they're going to be thinking about the cost and how long it will take more than anything else.

Various Other Supplies That You'll Need

You're obviously going to need more than just a box truck in order to move effectively. If all you had was a box truck, you technically could execute a move, however it's not going to be successful. There's a high probability that items are going to be damaged along the way. So here are some of the other supplies that you'll need to start this business:

Moving Pads and Shrink Wrap

Moving pads or moving blankets are going to be essential for any move you complete. They aren't like a normal blanket; instead, they're thicker, more sturdy, and designed for moving. They'll help to protect items you move from scratches and other such damage that could occur when you're moving items.

Moving blankets are essentially a one time expense. You're going to have to buy enough to get you started, and you'll only need more as you expand or if one gets damaged. The other supply you're going to need is shrink wrap.

It comes in a large size and a smaller size, both of which are handy for different situations. Let's say you're going to move a couch. You could put a moving pad on the ground and then stand the couch on top of the pad. You'd then fold the excess of the pad up around the sofa and then use large shrink wrap around the entire couch.

If the couch has extra pillows that fall off when the couch is in a vertical position, then keep the couch horizontal and place the pad around the end that will be on the ground when it's in the vertical position. Once the pad is in place, use shrink to wrap up the couch while it's still in the horizontal position. Now if the size allows for it, you can use a two wheel dolly to move the couch around with ease without having to worry about your dolly scraping, scratching, or getting dirt on the customers couch.

You can also stand up the couch vertically in your truck to save space and not have to worry about damage. If you're dealing with a smaller item that you need to stay in tact, you can use the handheld or smaller shrink wrap to hold the item together and make it easy for transport. Essentially, every item that's moved needs to be secured in some way shape or form, so you're going to use a lot of pads and a lot of shrink.

Boxes of Various Sizes

Ideally, the customer should have everything boxed up as much as possible and be ready to go when you arrive. You'll come to realize that this won't happen as often as you'd like, and you'll be the one boxing things up. This isn't an issue as you can charge the customer for the boxes you have to use, and it will make the move take longer, so it's more money for your business.

This is why you always need to be prepared and have a variety of different box sizes on hand at all times. Boxes are essential because you can pack a lot of different items in them and they are easy to stack which makes them super clutch for packing in a truck.

When it comes to charging a customer, keep it simple and charge them twice the amount that you paid for the box. So for example, if you used a box that you spent $2.50 on, then you would charge the customer $5 for that box.

Straps

You have to use straps to keep things in place in your box truck. Imagine the headboard to a bed frame. If you lay it down, it's taking up too much space in your truck. If you keep it vertical, then it has the potential of falling down and being damaged.

This is where you'd use straps to keep something such as a headboard firmly in place against the wall. Again, this is where something like moving blankets are essential because you can put the blanket over the headboard, and now it's protected from scrapes from your strap or the wall of your truck. You also need straps to keep stacked boxes in place.

You want to fully maximize the space you have in your truck, and one of the best ways you can do that is by stacking boxes on top of each other.

The only problem with stacking is the potential for that stack to topple over if you hit your brakes suddenly, which will definitely happen if you're on the road long enough. Straps will keep stacked boxes tightly in place and help give you peace of mind when you're driving the truck.

Packaging Tape

Another item you're consistently going to have to buy is packaging tape. This will primarily be used to tape your boxes shut. The best way to use packaging tape is with a handheld tape dispenser.

This will allow you to easily tear the tape when you need to. It can be difficult to rip packaging tape with your hands, so this tool will definitely come in handy out in the field.

Box Cutters

Box cutters will be another supply item you'll constantly use to complete a move. You'll need to rip through packaging tape and cut through shrink wrap for the most part. You'll just want to be careful when cutting through your shrink wrap and tape because you don't want to accidentally cut into the customer's item.

An easy way to prevent this from happening is to pull the shrink wrap towards you. This will keep the wrap tight making it easier to cut, and it will ensure you have space between the item and the wrap so that your blade doesn't come into contact with the item.

Power Drills, Various Tool Bits, and Basic Tool Kit

You'll want to have some basic tools with you on the job in case you have to disassemble an item in order to be able to move it. A common example of a piece you'll need to disassemble before loading would be a bed frame. It simply isn't going to be practical to move an item like that without taking it apart first.

If you show up without tools, you'll look very unprofessional in front of the customer. Having a power drill with various tool bits and a basic tool kit will have you prepared for just about anything you come across.

2 Wheel and 4 Wheel Dollies

Dollies will make your moving life way easier. That goes without saying, but you'll definitely want to get a 2 wheel and a couple of 4 wheel dollies at a minimum. 2 wheel dollies are great because of their height, which makes them easy to use.

The downside is that they're not great for bulky items that contain a lot of length and width. This is where your 4 wheel dollies come into play. They're going to be much more effective for moving large and bulky items.

The reason why you'll want at least two is for those items you may come across that are extra large. Rather than using one dolly in the middle and having the item be unstable, you can place one dolly on each end of the item to allow for an easy move. There is one big pro tip for using a 4 wheel dolly.

Let's say you're moving a dresser; place the dolly on one side of the dresser at a 45 degree angle. Then start to tilt the dresser towards the dolly while keeping the dolly at 45 degrees.

When the side of the dresser comes in contact with the dolly, you can start to lower the dolly until it is parallel to the floor. This is an easy way to get bulky items onto your dolly without them being awkwardly placed to where they're constantly tipping over causing you to get frustrated.

Moving Straps

Moving straps are long straps that are meant to help you move mattresses. The straps will be secured on both of your arms and then the middle of the strap will be underneath the mattress so the strap essentially forms a U-shape.

Your partner will do the same thing on the other side of the mattress, and the straps will make it a lot easier to carry items like mattresses. Speaking of mattresses, this is why it's a good idea to carry mattress bags with you as well to prevent a mattress from getting dirty during the move.

A Moving Partner

Completing a move on your own simply isn't going to work. You're going to come across too many common household items that will require two people to move. This is especially true when stairs are involved.

You're not going to be able to use dollies to carry certain big bulky items up and down stairs. You're going to have to manually carry certain items, and in order to do that, you're going to need a moving partner. If you form this business as a partnership, then that's great; you already have a partner who can help you out.

What if you're starting this business by yourself and need someone else to help you out in the beginning? The first place I recommend you look is with your immediate friends and family. Do you know of anyone who might be willing to help you out that you think you might work well with?

If no one comes to mind, make a post on your personal social media accounts and see if you gain any interest. Your next escalation from there is going to be to post an online ad on a job website to look for candidates. The topic of growing your business will be covered more in depth later on, but for now the main thing you need to know is that you want to initially hire someone as a contractor and not as an employee.

The reason for this is so that you can use your moving partner on an as needed basis. With an employee, you'll have to pay the person for consistent hours and the work simply might not be there in the beginning to justify that. By hiring someone as a contractor, you give yourself the ability to only pay them on an as needed basis.

Creating the Business

Now that I've covered what supplies you'll need, let's go over some things you'll need to do to actually create your business. The first thing you'll need to do is come up with a name, which will usually involve something followed by the word movers or moving. Including the word movers or moving as part of your name is a good idea because it lets people know exactly what your company does.

Your name doesn't need to be anything groundbreaking, it can be simple. When you're creating a business, there are a lot of things you have to do to get things off the ground. You don't want to spend weeks sitting there trying to come up with the perfect name.

Once you do come up with a name, now it's time to think about the type of business entity that you want to establish. You have C corp, S corp, LLC, partnership, and sole proprietorship. Which one is right for your business?
To answer that, you have to consider what your goals are. There's a reason why the biggest companies in the world are C corporations. However, that doesn't mean that a C corporation is inherently the right choice for you.

Look at some of the biggest companies in the world, and you'll see that they aren't moving companies. That shouldn't bother you one bit because there's still plenty of money to be made in this industry. On the other end of the spectrum, you have a sole proprietorship.

A sole proprietorship is the simplest type of entity, but it has a big downside. The downside is that it doesn't offer you any protection. With an LLC, you get protection in case your company ends up in a lawsuit.

It will be more expensive to establish and maintain when compared to a sole proprietorship, but the benefits are worth it. Again, you have to think about the industry that you're in. You're a moving company, and things can happen.

A customer could claim that you damaged their walls even though they were already damaged before you started the move. Ultimately, the decision is yours to make, but I recommend that you establish an entity that can offer you protection. The other option you have is to form a partnership.

This is a good option to consider since you'll need someone else to help you out in the field.

You won't have to worry about getting help every time you have a move. You and your partner can work together and possibly be able to build the business up to a higher level faster than you could do on your own.

You could find a partner who makes up for your weaknesses. For example, maybe you have a lot of in field experience with moving, but your weakness is marketing. Your partner could be someone who is good at marketing to help sure up your downside.

You'd want to make sure though that this person can at least be competent in the field. If not, you're going to have a tough time. The downside, of course, to a partnership is that you'll have to share profits with your partner as well, which is something you may not want to worry about.

You also have to consider putting in equal amounts of effort into the business as well. You don't want to be putting in all of the work just for your partner to be lazy and ride your coattail.

How Risky Do You Want to Get?

Up next on the list is going to be insurance. Starting a moving company without insurance is not a wise idea. There are a few things you're going to want to get insurance for.

First and foremost, you will need insurance for your box truck. Aside from that, what other types of insurance should you consider? The main one is going to be general liability insurance.

If you're in this industry for a long enough time period, something unfortunate could happen and you need to be prepared. You could be moving an item and it wrecks a wall or dings the side of the customers car. You're obviously not going to do anything like that on purpose, but accidents definitely happen out in the field.

An insurance policy can help cover damages that may occur while you're working. Another type of insurance you'll eventually need to consider is workers' compensation insurance. If your goal is to grow to the point where you're operating multiple trucks and have multiple teams out in the field at once, you're going to need workers' compensation insurance.

If one of your employees gets hurt on the job, then workers' compensation insurance can help to cover medical expenses and wages for the employee. Workers' compensation insurance isn't going to be cheap, but consider again the industry you're in. Your workers are going to consistently be moving items.

People are going to be moving backwards and could trip over something. People are going to be moving up and down stairs with bulky and heavy items. Injury is a very realistic possibility that you need to be prepared for when you start hiring movers. You also need to consider getting cargo insurance which will help to cover items that are damaged or lost during transit.

Do You Need a USDOT Number?

Depending on how and where you operate your business will determine if you need a USDOT number. Certain states don't require a USDOT number if you stay within the state. If you're crossing states lines, you're going to need to get a number.

Most states require a USDOT number even if your business is purely intrastate. As a moving company, you're definitely going to get customers wanting to do long distance moves who are moving from one state to another. Therefore, I recommend that you go ahead and get registered.

The same type of premise goes for an MC number. If you're crossing state lines, you're going to need an MC number. So go ahead and get one to ensure you're ready for any job that comes your way. The last thing you want is to have to turn down a job because you don't have the proper proceedings set up.

Chapter 3: How to Land Jobs to Keep Things Moving

By this point in the book, you can set up your business. What fun is it though to get everything set up just to sit there and twiddle your thumbs? You need jobs so that you can keep things moving like you're supposed to do.

So how do you go about doing that? There's so many different ways out there that you could market your company that you're likely going to get overwhelmed thinking about the possibilities.

After reading this chapter, you'll have a good understanding as to how you should approach marketing. You can't do everything, so you need to focus on what matters most.

Small Fish in a Big Pond

The very first thing that I want you to understand is that when you first start off, you're likely going to be a small fish in a big pond. What I mean by this is that you're going to have some competition right out of the gate from established companies that you're going to have to compete with. This may not be the case if you're in a more remote location, but chances are good that you're going to be dealing with some established companies.

Don't panic at the thought of this. There are pros and cons to being big and there are pros and cons to being small. You simply have to take advantage of the strengths that come with being a smaller company.

Therefore, you have to be smart with your approach. You simply can't tackle things the same way the bigger companies do. They have way more reviews than you do.

People will be more trusting of a name they've heard before when compared to someone new. People want to go with a company they can trust, which makes sense. However, hiring a moving company isn't exactly cheap.

People need to be able to afford the service, which means you could offer better pricing as a way to be competitive. Your overhead costs will be lower than an established company, so you can still make a good profit from your moving jobs. How to price your service will be covered in depth in the next chapter, but for right now, hopefully you understand the mentality behind how you should be approaching things.

Think about it from the perspective of a potential customer. They're interested in hiring a moving company, but they don't know who they should go with. You have to think about why someone should choose you over anyone else in the area.

In order for someone to choose you, they first and foremost have to know who you are. With that in mind, what are some things you can do to ensure you're exposing your business to the right people?

Drop off Flyers or Business Cards at Apartment Complexes

When you're starting out, you need ways to effectively market your company that aren't super expensive. In order to do that, you have to think creatively. One way to do that is to target people that live in apartments.

The reason for this is because people who live in an apartment are renters who will typically sign a 12-month lease. Some people might be on a longer or shorter lease, but a year is pretty standard. This means if you're able to get in front of these people, you'll likely get some people who are about to move out or who will be moving out in a couple of months.

Yes, someone could resign their lease, however things change. Rent could be going up and the person needs to move to a cheaper complex. Someone could be moving into a house.

Someone might need to move because of a job change. You simply don't know what someone's situation is, but if they're in an apartment, there's a chance they could be moving soon. The best way to be able to do this is to create a simple flyer or business card and then leave it at everyone's door.

Typically, apartment doors will have a little clip next to each door that you can hang your business card or flyer on. If not, you can simply wedge the flyer or card in between the door and the frame.

Before doing this, you'll simply want to check with the apartment complex to ensure you're good to go. If you do this at enough places, you'll have a good chance of reaching people when they're about to move out, so do this as much as you possibly can.

Yard Signs

I'm sure you've seen yard signs randomly in a city before or in a neighborhood to help lead people to a yard sale. You might be thinking, "What good is a yard sign going to do?" It's totally reasonable to think that way because placing a yard sign just anywhere isn't going to yield great results.

It all comes down to placement. In the case of a moving company, what's a place you can target where you know people will be moving? You could target new residential areas that are being built.

People will be checking out these new homes and buying them, which means that they'll be moving from their old place to this new residential area. So if you're able to place a yard sign somewhere in the area, it can be highly effective to bring in new customers. Another area you can consider is colleges.

Most dorm rooms are going to come furnished, but you could definitely market around nearby apartments. Some of them will be furnished and some won't be. You'll definitely want to target the apartments that aren't furnished.

You might think that this isn't worth your time because college students typically don't have a lot of extra money. This is true, however you're not worried about college students paying you, it's most likely going to be their parents. There are going to be parents who don't want to deal with the hassle of moving their kid into a new apartment, so this is where you come into play.

You simply want to check with the city to ensure you get a permit if necessary to put your sign in a public area. If you want to know how effective this marketing effort is for your business, you need a way to track the data. The best way you can do this is by putting a unique promo code on the yard sign that people can use.

So for example, you could put "Use promo code yardsign10 to receive a 10% discount on your move." This way when someone contacts you and uses the promo code yardsign10, you'll know the business was generated from that yard sign. You could create a unique promo code for each yard sign that you put out so that you can gauge the effectiveness in a certain area.

You can also do this for the apartments as well. You can create a code for the flyer or business card and use a different code for each apartment complex if you want to. The best way to do this would be to create a few different designs with the only difference being the code.

You could then split the amount you print between the variations. So for example, let's say you wanted 1,000 business cards. You could create 5 different promos and print 200 of each variation instead of 1,000 of one single variation.

Be a Moving Billboard

Since you're a moving company, your truck is going to be out on the road quite a bit. Why not make the most of your time out on the road and continually advertise to new people? You can do this by getting your box truck wrapped to promote your company.

You can put your company's name and contact information on the 3 main sides of the truck to help increase visibility. Getting a box truck is going to cost you a pretty penny though because there's a lot of surface area that needs to be covered. It very easily will cost thousands of dollars to get your box truck wrapped. So you have to consider where you're at in your business.

If you don't have a lot of jobs right now, then it probably does you no good to get your truck wrapped if it's not out on the road. That money could be better spent somewhere else in the beginning. However, as time goes on and you have more moving jobs consistently, you could be missing out on business by not having your company information on the sides and back of your box truck.

Initially though, don't feel as if this is something that you have to do. A customer is going to book you based on other factors and they're not going to immediately cancel the job if they see you pull up in a box truck that's unmarked. Your truck will be able to get them moved all the same, which is why you have to make the decision that's best for your business.

We Live in the Digital Age

The present day is the digital age. The internet changed everything. It allowed us to communicate with each other faster and easier than ever before.

And of course, we have to talk about social media. Social media changed the way people do business. So in this day and age, you're missing out if your business is not on social media.

People will want to check out your presence on social media. They'll check your website (I'll get to that in a bit). People do these things because they want to make sure the company is legit before they hire them.

Think about if someone heard of your business, but they couldn't find your business on social media or the internet? How do you think that would make them feel? Well, let me put it to you this way; how would you feel if you couldn't find a company's website, they don't have any social media accounts, and they have no online presence whatsoever?

Would you be hesitant about doing business with that company? Would you have second thoughts? Would you start researching others companies?

I'd be willing to bet that you'd consider paying more to go with a company that does have an online presence because it's easier to trust them. So yes, social media is critical, but you might not have a clue as to how you should be approaching social media. Hopefully, I can break things down for you in a simple way.

What Platforms and How Much?

The first thing you have to decide on is what platforms you should utilize. You likely already have personal social media accounts that you use, so I recommend sticking to platforms that you're familiar and comfortable with. My biggest piece of advice is to not bite off more than you can chew.

What I mean by that is that it may sound tempting to get on every single social media channel there is. While that may sound good in theory, you have to realize that you have a lot on your plate as the owner of a moving company. You're going to be doing a lot of different things, and you simply might not be able to keep up with every current platform.

Yes, it would be the best case scenario to be on every platform, but don't put that pressure on yourself. Instead, go with bite-sized chunks that you can handle. You can always build up your appetite, so to speak, over time.

For you, maybe you feel comfortable with three different platforms because that's what you're comfortable with. Maybe you think that you can only handle one platform. Either way is totally fine.

It's less about the number of platforms and more about what you do on the platforms that you are using. So with that in mind, how often should you post content? This is another best case scenario type of thing.

Ideally, you would be posting multiple times a day for each social media account that you have. While that may be optimal, once again, that likely isn't going to be sustainable for you, at least not in the beginning. So start with what you're comfortable with, and build your way up.

Initially, you might only post 2 times per week. As time goes on, try to steadily build your way up to posting once per day. Posting that often may sound great and all, but what kind of content should you post? Well, here are some ideas:

Tips About How to Move

You might think that giving away your best moving secrets is a bad idea because it will encourage people to want to do the job themselves. That's a totally reasonable thought, but you have to keep in mind that even with the best tricks of the trade, moving can still be a challenge.

It simply won't matter if someone knows how to optimally move, they still won't want to do it. However, by posting tips, you're essentially flexing your knowledge and letting your followers see that you know your stuff. It's less about teaching others and more so about demonstrating your knowledge.

This will help to build trust with your audience because they'll get to see proof that you know what you're doing out in the field. Here are a few post ideas you could post about this topic:

-How to get couches through doorframes effectively

-The right technique to lift an item so that you don't strain your lower back

-How to properly carry an item up stairs (This is a great post because it will remind people with stairs what they'll have to go through if they want to complete their move themselves)

-How long a move should take

-How long it should take to pack up your home (Posts like this are awesome because it will make people realize how long it's going to take, and they may not want to move themselves for that long of a time)

-What size box truck to complete a move in one fell swoop (This type of post can be reused multiple times. For example, what size box truck would you need to move a 600 square foot apartment in one fell swoop? Next month, you could make the same post except for a 2,000 square foot house. You just want to give averages here, and talk about how things can vary based on how much stuff you have. The main point with these types of posts is to give people a better understanding of what it's going to take to get moved.)

Different Supplies to Execute a Move

Another topic you can post about are the different supplies you use for a job that could be helpful for others. Most people won't have a clue about the different supplies they could use to help them with their move. This is where you can come in and establish yourself as an authority by showing people different tools for the job and how to use them. Here are a few ideas:

-Showing people how to get bulky items onto a 4 wheel dolly by yourself

-How to properly wrap an item to keep it safe from scratches and dents while moving it

-How to use moving blankets

-How to use mattress straps

-How to take the feet off of a couch to get it to fit through a doorframe

-The most common drill bits you use during a move

-When to use small stretch wrap vs. large stretch wrap

-When to use a 2-wheel dolly opposed to a 4-wheel dolly

Make Posts While You're on the Job

Another good idea is to make posts while you're on the job. You can film quick 15-30 second videos of yourself or your crew on the job and show them various aspects of it. It doesn't have to be anything fancy.

It could be carrying something bulky up the stairs. It could be an intriguing video such as, "do you think we'll be able to fit this item through this doorframe?" It could be a quick video of you driving to a job or what you eat for lunch when you're constantly on the road. Be fun and creative with this because you want to show people aspects of your personal side.

You want to let people know who you are outside of your moving company and what your personality is like on the job. Making a post while you're on the job is great because jobs will be different every time, and this gives you the opportunity to easily create content without having to think much about it.

Questions You Get Asked a Ton of Times

You can also make posts answering questions that you get asked a ton of times. Even if you don't get asked something a lot, it's still a good idea to make posts based on common problems you know people will run into. You could make some posts such as the following:

-Do I need to box everything before the moving team arrives?

-What else can the customer do to help prepare for the move?

-What should the customer do during the move?

-How far in advance should I call to make an appointment?

-How much will it cost? (This can be a good one because people generally don't like to call to get pricing. If you're up front with your pricing and your pricing is good, people will be more likely to go with your moving company.)

-How long will it take?

Cool Story Bro

In the moving industry, you'll definitely come across some interesting pieces that you've moved or you'll just have interesting stories to tell in general. Post about some of the things you've come across while out in the field or other crazy stories that have happened.

Blunders on the Job

Talk about blunders that have happened or can happen while on a move and how they can be prevented. It can be from your own personal experience.

You may think that it's not a good idea to share your own mistakes, but this will show your human side. As long as you share what you learned from it and how things are different now because of it, you don't have anything to worry about. Here are a few examples:

-How to avoid scraping your wall while moving

-How to ensure you're packing a truck correctly so you don't have leftover items

-The time I broke an item and how you can do things differently

Connect with Real Estate Agents

Another thing you can do on social media is connect with real estate agents in your local area. The reason why this is so important is because real estate agents are selling homes. People have to move into those homes from another place, right?

So if you can make the right connections and offer a good incentive, you can get real estate agents to help give recommendations for your company. It doesn't need to be anything complicated either. You can like and comment on their posts.

Give them a follow. You can easily find where they hang out by looking at relevant hashtags such as #SanDiegoRealEstate. As for an incentive, offer them 15% of the total move price for each customer they send you.

The reason why you want to do this is because it's unlikely that you'll have real estate agents recommend your business for no reason. However, if they can make money from it and someone is moving anyways, then they'll be way more likely to suggest your company. You can simply direct message real estate agents and ask a general question to start the conversation such as the following:

-How long have you been selling real estate?

-What made you want to get into real estate?

-What's the biggest sized house you've sold before?

You want to keep the conversation focused on them. People will usually check out your profile, and they'll see that you operate a moving company. They might ask you a similar question back such as why you started a moving company.

You'll definitely want to answer their question, but you can use this as an opportunity to transition into telling them about your referral program. Aside from direct messaging real estate agents, you can make a general post about your referral bonus and simply use relevant hashtags such as #realestate or #SanDiegoRealEstate to ensure that real estate agents in your area see the post.

Yes, your followers will see the post as well, and that's completely okay. You may receive some referrals from your followers as well, which is a good thing. Targeting real estate agents for this will be more effective though because they're going to be consistently interacting with people who are moving.

Building Your Online Presence

As I previously mentioned, having a presence online is very important, not just with social media, but also with an online website. People are going to judge you if you don't have a website. They're also going to judge you if your website looks bad.

Your competition is going to have websites, and their websites are going to look good, so you need to follow suit. The last thing you want is to miss out on business because you don't have a website. You might not know a lot about tech, coding, or how to build your own website from scratch in a way that looks professional.

That's totally okay. You can outsource this project to someone else so that you can focus on other things. Hiring someone to design a website for you is likely going to cost a couple grand if you want it done right by an experienced professional.

You can likely hire someone for cheaper who's just starting out. That may be worth the risk if you want to try to save some money. Either way, you'll be able to work with this person on what your vision is for the design and overall feel of your website.

As they're creating it, you can tell them what you like and what you don't like. Look at some of your competitors' websites and see what stands out to you.

Also, take a close look at what you think is missing so that you can stand out from the crowd. Yes, a website may be a tough pill to swallow cost wise, but it's an investment that will pay for itself time and again.

Go Hard Year Round

Some of the last advice that I want to give you is to go hard year round. When it comes to moving, the summer months are typically busier than the winter months. Just because there's less demand during winter doesn't mean that your company has to be slow.

Some companies have the mindset of, "oh well things will just be slow because it's winter." They won't push as hard during those months to get new customers. You want to take the opposite approach from that mindset.

You want to go hard year round and do your best to bring in new customers. Go hard on social media and pass out your flyers and business cards as much as possible. Do this year round and you'll be amazed at the results.

Don't fall into the negative mindset just because it's a certain month. People are still going to need movers, so do your best to expose your business to them!

Chapter 4: Determining What You Need to Charge

What you charge for your services is a very critical aspect of your business. Getting paid is obviously how you're going to pay your bills and keep things going, so it's very important to nail this step. There are a lot of factors that play into what you determine your rate is.

Remember that nothing has to be set in stone. This is a benefit of being a smaller company. People aren't going to notice if your prices change.

So think of your prices in the beginning as a fluid thing. It's capable of changing if you need it to; you're not locked into anything. After reading this chapter though, you'll have a good understanding as to what you should charge for your moving services.

What Should You Charge Per Hour?

Most moving companies are going to charge customers by the hour. So if a move takes six hours, the customer is going to be billed for six hours. If the company charges $100 per hour, the customer is going to be charged $600, and that's not including any other fees that may be added on such as if you have to supply the customer with boxes.

Established moving companies will typically charge anywhere from $100-$250 per hour. This rate is largely dependent upon where you live and how many movers are being used. Typically, people will hire two movers and they'll have one truck.

However, people can order one truck with three movers, or they can even hire multiple trucks with multiple movers for each truck. So for instance, someone could hire three trucks with two movers for each truck for a total of six movers. The hourly rate will increase with each truck and driver that goes out.

In my area, you'll see about $100-$150 per hour for one box truck with two movers. The good news is that in the beginning, you don't have to worry about managing a giant fleet with multiple trucks and drivers. You're going to set a standard rate for your single truck with two movers.

So let's say, for the sake of example, you determine the average rate for a moving company in your area is $100-$150 per hour for one box truck and two movers. How should you price your services accordingly? Well, I need to bring it back to a point I mentioned earlier; why should someone choose you?

You're starting out, so play to your strengths. One of those strengths is lower overhead costs. You don't have to manage a truck fleet like other companies do.

You don't have to hire multiple positions to operate like other companies do. You don't have the same insurance costs like established companies do. Don't get me wrong; if you're interested in expanding, you will have these same expenses eventually.

For right now though, your costs to operate your business on a day-to-day basis are much lower. If you charge the same as everyone else, you're going to lose because you're not playing to your strengths. With all of this in mind, I'd charge anywhere between $60-$75 per hour for the moving service for one box truck and two movers.

This price point is a good chunk cheaper than the average so people will definitely take that into consideration when choosing a moving company. It's also not so low that people wonder if your company is too good to be true. The price point is still legitimate enough to make sense for a business to offer.

I'm not saying that you need to blindly pick a number between $60-75 and charge that. Do some research for moving company prices in your area. Also, take into consideration what your current expenses are to operate your business, as this will vary.

Take all of that and factor it in to help you determine your price point. What I want you to understand is that you need to be priced cheaper when compared to other established companies in your area. This will allow you to even the playing field because you're playing to your strengths as a smaller company.

What Should I Charge for an Extra Mover?

So for example, let's say that you settle on $70 per hour for one box truck and two movers. At the start, this is likely all that you'll have to offer because you'll probably have one truck and one other person helping you out. As you start to expand though, how should your pricing change?

Once again, it's hard to give you a set in stone price. There are going to be varying factors that come into play that can change how much extra you should charge someone. Let's start off with the most basic example, which would be adding one additional person to the crew for a specific move.

It's obviously going to be easier to add an extra person as a contractor for one move when compared to having to buy a whole extra truck. So if a customer requests an extra person, how much more should you charge? Keep in mind that you don't have to bring along a third person if you don't feel like it's necessary.

Your company can offer only two movers and leave it at that. You could also suggest a third mover to the customer if you feel like the situation calls for it. The thing you have to keep in mind is the overall cost of the move.

For example, let's say you're charging $70 per hour, and you estimate that it's going to take five hours for two people to execute the move. The cost for the customer is going to be $350. If you add in an extra person, the hourly rate will go up, but the amount of time it takes to complete the move will go down.

Therefore, if you don't increase the hourly rate by an appropriate amount, then you'll end up losing money. For example, let's say you bring on a third person and charge the customer an extra $25 per hour for the extra hands. You're paying the helper $15 an hour, so your margins are still good in that regard.

However, the job now only takes 3.5 hours instead of five hours to complete. The customer is charged $95 an hour for 3.5 hours for a grand total of $332.50, which is a total of $17.50 less than you would have made if you just used two people. So how much should you charge?

Generally speaking, rates can increase by an extra $30-$35 per hour for a third mover to come along. If we used the example from above, this range would work out well. If you charged an extra $30 per hour, that would come out to $350 for 3.5 hours of work, which is the same overall amount for two movers at $70 per hour.

So how do you know when you should use a third mover as opposed to just two? The first scenario would be a customer request. A customer might have urgency with their move; let's say they need it completed as fast as possible.

The other scenario you should consider is how busy you are. If the price point remains about the same overall, you might think there isn't much of a benefit to adding in the third person. The reason why it can be extremely helpful is because it's saving you time and you're still making the same amount of money.

This means that you can move to the next job quicker. So if you're slammed, book an extra person so you can fit more jobs on your schedule. If you're slow, don't worry about adding in the third person.

In the case where it's to your benefit to add in the third person, remember you control the narrative with the customer. You can tell them that you estimate the move to take five hours with two people or around 3.5 hours with three people so they'll spend the same amount, it'll just take less time. Most people will be fine with this, and it will allow you to schedule more jobs.

What Should I Charge for an Extra Truck?

Here's the typical progression for increasing workload for a move:

-Two movers and one box truck
-Three movers and one box truck
-Two box trucks with 4 movers
-Two box trucks with 5 movers
-Two box trucks with 6 movers etc.

You'll obviously be executing a pretty big move if you're needing multiple box trucks, but it definitely happens because some people have a lot of stuff in a big house. When it comes to adding in an extra box truck, how much more should you charge the customer? This is much easier to determine as you'll simply double your normal rate.

So if you charge $70 for one box truck with two movers, then you'll charge $140 per hour for two box trucks with four movers. If a fifth mover is needed, then you'll tack on the extra rate; if we use the example from above, that's an extra $30. So in this case, that would be a rate of $170 per hour for two trucks and five movers.

Once you get your initial rates set, adding in an extra box truck isn't tricky to calculate. Yes, you are going to have to do some legwork to figure out your sweet spot for pricing, but it's essential for you to have a successful moving company.

Keep in mind too, as I mentioned earlier, the first price you come up with isn't set in stone. You can adjust it as you do more jobs and start to realize that you might be charging too little or too much.

Should You Require an Hour Minimum?

Something that's common in the moving industry is to require an hour minimum. For example, a moving company might require a minimum of three hours in order for them to accept the job. So if that company charges $100 per hour, they're basically saying that we have to charge a minimum of $300 in order for this job to be worth our time.

That's totally reasonable given that they probably have a lot of jobs to deal with, and they want to weed out the smaller jobs that simply won't be worth their time or won't be as profitable. You can definitely do the same and require a minimum number of hours, but why not be different? You need ways to separate yourself from other moving companies.

Imagine someone doesn't have a lot of items and they live in a small one bedroom apartment.

Let's say the estimated move is 1.5 hours for two people with one truck. This person could very well go with your company simply because you're the only one who will take on the job.

A job is a job, right? Why not take what you can get? Your hourly rate should be high enough to where you're profitable no matter how many hours a job takes.

Again, play to your strengths as a smaller moving company. It might not be worth a larger company's time unless the customer pays for three hours of work that only takes 1.5 hours, which simply isn't a good deal for the customer. You can come in and charge them for only 1.5 hours of work.

You'll land the job, get paid, and the customer will be very delighted. As time goes on and you get bigger, you can always reconsider your position on this. In the beginning, I would recommend against doing this to help increase the chances of landing smaller jobs.

What if a Customer Doesn't Answer?

Another issue you'll run into is having an appointment set up with a customer, and when you get to their residence, no one answers! It can be extremely frustrating to say the least. Here you are booking someone and spending your time driving out there just for them to not answer.

It can happen for a multitude of different reasons. The customer might have slept in and isn't hearing your knocks or their doorbell ringing. The customer might have forgotten about the appointment or thought it was at a different time.

There could have been a communication issue between partners or roommates, and neither person is there. Someone leaves for a quick errand or different appointment and isn't back as quickly as they thought they would be. Or people need to cancel for one reason or another, but they don't call you; instead, they just ghost you.

All of these are very plausible scenarios that can cause someone to not answer the door when you show up. So what should you do if you find yourself in this situation? First, do all that you can to prevent this from happening in the first place.

You will need to make sure that you send a reminder text to the customer the day before their appointment to remind them about their move and have them confirm their appointment. This alone can help to prevent a lot of no-shows from happening. It can save a lot of time because you won't have to wait on the customer to scramble to get ready to answer the door.

You can also send a text once you leave giving the customer an estimate for when you'll arrive. Still though, let's say you get there and no one answers, what do you do? You can definitely knock or ring the doorbell multiple times.

Sometimes, people simply don't hear it or they need some time to get to the door. If they don't answer after a few minutes, then you'll want to go ahead and give them a call. They might answer and say they need to get ready or something else and that they'll be down in a few minutes.

That's totally cool. What if they answer, say they ran an errand, and it'll be 30 minutes until they get home. In a case like this, let them know that the clock has already started for their hourly rate.

So let's say the move actually starts at 8:30 am and ends at noon. The customer is going to be charged for four hours not 3.5 hours. You're the one who showed up on time and used your gas to get there.

You also might be on a time crunch. You might not be able to afford to wait around for 30 minutes in order to get started. Your company shouldn't have to take a hit because the customer wasn't available.

Let's talk about the other possibility, which is the customer isn't answering their phone or their door. How should you go about handling this? Your company should implement a 30 minute wait time for the customer to respond.

If they don't respond, then leave the job. Same premise here, it's not fair for your company to suffer simply because a customer is flaky or unorganized. Implement a no-show policy where the customer is charged for one hour if your company shows up and the customer is unresponsive.

Many companies implement policies similar to this. For example, a dentist office might require you to cancel your appointment with at least 24 hours notice or else you'll be charged a $25 cancellation fee. Cancellations and no-shows are frustrating no doubt, but it's even more so the case in the moving world because of gas.

It's not just your time that's being wasted, it's also the cost of gas for no extra benefit. In the beginning, you may not feel comfortable enforcing these policies. If you don't feel comfortable doing this, that's up to you.

When you're starting out, a cancellation might not be as impactful as it would be to an established company depending on how you look at things. For an established company, that's another job that's being missed out on because the customer isn't being responsive. A certain amount of hours were being blocked off of the schedule for a customer to essentially cancel without communicating that to the company.

It's an annoying aspect of the business to have to deal with, but it is what it is. Having these kinds of protocols in place can help to better protect you when it does unfortunately happen.

Put Your Money Where Your Mouth Is

You should also require the customer to put down a deposit in order to book an appointment with your company. This is a very common business practice, and it requires people to commit to using your company. Someone can easily act interested on the phone, book a move with you, and ghost you with no real repercussion.

Making a customer put down a deposit makes the customer prove to you that they're serious about using your company. You can also make the deposit non refundable as well. You should definitely make your deposit non refundable because what's the point of putting down a deposit if someone can mistreat you and then just get their money back?

The deposit is there to protect your company's time. So how large should you make the deposit? I recommend making the customer put down a deposit for the first hour of the move.

So if you charge $70 per hour, the customer must put down a $70 deposit in order to book a time with your company. This ties back into my previous point about no-shows. If you get the $70 as a deposit and the customer ignores you, then you don't have to worry about enforcing that no-show policy by sending an invoice, which the customer is unlikely to pay.
Instead, you basically already required the customer to pay the no-show fee upfront as a deposit in case something like a no-show happens. The other option you have for a deposit

is to charge them a percentage of the estimated cost of the job. Doing this is tricky for a couple of reasons.

The job could go faster than expected, and the deposit ends up being larger than the cost of the total job. This is an edge case scenario, but it can happen depending on what size the deposit is and how off the estimate is. The other problem is you have to calculate the remainder of the payment due every time.

It's not a simple calculation like it is with the other method. For example, let's say you require a one hour deposit of $70, and the total amount of time the job took ends up being 7 hours. The total cost for the job is $490, and you'd simply subtract the $70 deposit from the original $490; the customer would still owe you $420 at the end of the job.

The math is super simple every time. Regardless though, you can charge a percentage if you want to. Somewhere in the realm of 20% is a good bet because it's low enough to where you'll be unlikely to run into issues such as having to offer a partial refund because the job went faster than expected.

Giving Price Estimates

Giving price estimates in the moving industry is an absolute necessity. There are a few reasons for this. The first is that it will help your company budget its time properly.

It will let you know if you can fit in more jobs or if your schedule is full for that day. Secondly, it sets the expectation for the customer. A customer has no idea how long it's going to take for you to move them.

If you show up, get them moved, and drop the bill on them, they're likely going to be in shock of the cost. Big moves take a while, and the cost adds up. If a move takes 8 hours, you can bet that someone might be a little surprised by the total if they didn't know what to expect.

You can avoid this by giving a price estimate to the customer when they're on the phone with you. So how do you go about giving a price estimate? You want to ask the customer basic questions such as how many square feet their home is, how many bedrooms they have, do they have a shed or garage, how many people live in the home, and then you could ask some more questions about how much stuff they have.

The amount of things they have is where things get tricky. It's very hard to gauge the individual amount of items someone can own. You can likely expect a dining table and chairs in a kitchen or dining area.

You can assume there will be furniture in the living room and probably a mattress and dresser in a bedroom. What if someone just has a lot of stuff? Even if you try to ask specific questions, you still may not get the full picture. People, generally speaking, will try to lowball the amount of stuff they say they have.

The reason for this is simple; it will cause you to give a lower price estimate. This makes the customer think that their bill will be close to the amount that you estimated for them. However, the team will show up, it will definitely take longer, and now the customer feels justified to complain about how off the estimate was and that they shouldn't have to pay that much.

In these cases, the customer needs to realize that the job isn't going to go faster just because you tried to make it seem like you don't own that much stuff. During the conversation, you should also mention to the customer that they should have everything boxed up in advance that's possible. This will help save time on the job, and they won't have to buy boxes from you.

Even if you tell people this in advance, people will forget, or they simply might not care. Your team will have to box everything up, which hey, at least that means more money! Knowing this in advance, how can you combat this potential behavior with your customers?

Some people might do it on purpose and others by accident, but it's still something you need to avoid when possible. The best thing you can do is always overestimate the amount of time you think the job will take. A good rule of thumb is to estimate an extra hour for every two hours you think the job will take.

So if you originally think a job is going to take four hours, go ahead and say six hours. This way the customer won't be surprised, and you won't overbook yourself when the customer has more stuff than they led you to believe. Unfortunately, giving time estimates is just tricky.

There's no good way to go about it. As time goes on, you'll get a good grasp as to how fast your crew works, and you'll be able to give better estimates. Initially though, just communicate with the customer that this is an estimate, and things could take longer or less time than what you're estimating.

If you want to go the extra mile, you could have the customer use their phone to video chat you. This would allow you to visually see the layout of the home and get approximates for how much stuff they have. It still isn't perfect though as it's not realistic for them to go through every drawer and cabinet in their home, and things like sheds just get missed at times.

Plus, the customer might give you a call at work and might be unable to give you a tour of their home. If you communicate though and overestimate on the time you think it will take, then you shouldn't have many issues.

Gas Charges?

If you execute a long-distance move, you have to take gas into consideration. The reason for this is because it's going to cost you more money to complete this move because more time will be spent driving as opposed to actually moving. You'll also end up further away from your home base, which is more gas on your part.

You have to consider at what point you want to implement a gas charge. You don't need to include a gas charge for local moves, but if you're moving someone 50+ miles, you need to consider adding in a gas charge. Of course, it's your company so you can add in a gas charge for 75 or 100+ miles, if you wish.

Any of those options are reasonable depending on the area you live. How much should you charge for it? Well, first and foremost, they're only being charged for the extra amount.

So if you move people without a gas charge for up to 50 miles, and someone is moving 60 miles away, then a gas charge would only apply to 10 miles. I recommend doing something simple. Take the current price of gas in your area, which lets say is $4.50 for a gallon of diesel gas.

Next, you're going to divide that amount by the gas mileage your box truck gets. Box trucks don't get great gas mileage, so let's assume your truck gets 8 miles to the gallon. You'll then divide $4.50 by 8 to get 56 cents per gallon.

Then add 15 cents for maintenance such as oil changes. This means you'd charge the customer an extra 71 cents per mile that's over your limit. In this case, that's 10 extra miles for a total of $7.10.

Getting on the Same Page

The last thing you'll want to make sure you do is get the customer to sign and agree to your terms and conditions for the move. This will help to protect you in case disagreements pop up. You can easily send your form for the customer to sign via email, in which they could print, sign, scan, and send back to you.

If not, you can have the customer sign the form before you start the move; either option works great. There's even softwares you can use to have a customer electronically sign the document on their computer, which is another easy option as well. The following are some considerations for your customer agreement:

What You Won't Move

You need to be clear with the customer about what you will and will not move. Yes, you're a moving company and might feel desperate for jobs in the beginning, but there are things that are just too risky to handle. You could also come across items that are simply too large to be able to move if your initial crew is just you and one other person.

Some examples include guns, ammunition, gas cans, and propane tanks. Moving guns creates a safety problem in and of itself. You can't trust that the gun is unloaded even if the customer says it is.

Propane tanks and gas cans are fire hazards. The good news is that it's your company, and you get to set the standard for what you're not willing to move.

Hour Minimum, Deposit, Gas Charge, and Other Fees Such as Charging for Boxes

I talked about these more in depth previously, but you'll definitely want to include clauses regarding these matters. If not, you'll have no grounds to stand on if the customer disputes a certain charge.

Include the Price Estimate

When the customer signs, they're not agreeing to pay the estimated price; they're simply acknowledging what their price estimate is. This gives you something to go back to if the customer freaks out about the final price. You can show them the agreement they signed and show how the final cost ended up being cheaper.

If they are alarmed because the final cost was more than the estimate, you can explain to them why the job took longer than expected. For example, maybe the customer said everything would be boxed up upon arrival, but it wasn't.

Chapter 5: Tips for How to Properly Execute a Move Out in the Field

We've covered a lot of different aspects about a moving business so far that have related to getting things set up, marketing, etc. Now let's get into some tips for how you can better execute a move out in the field. Maybe you've already worked for a moving company in the past or maybe you haven't.

Either way, I think you'll find great value from this chapter. You don't want to put yourself or a team member at a high risk for injury. That will just set you back because an injured person won't be able to complete a job.

Make Sure You Are Top Notch at This

First and foremost, you want to ensure that you provide exceptional customer service when you're interacting with customers. The main reason for this is because moving is stressful for people. They might be on a time crunch, they might be moving into their first home, and they might have a thousand other things going on.

It's your job to help keep them calm and ensure that the move goes as smoothly as possible. Moving is strenuous, and it certainly can be hard at times to have a good attitude, but you don't want to let it show. This will easily lead to negative feedback from the customer, which will have a huge impact on how others view your company.

As long as you show up on time, have a good attitude, are friendly and personable, and answer any questions to calm someone's nerves then you have nothing to worry about. Those things may sound really basic, but you'd be surprised by how often they get overlooked.

Do This Upon Arrival

When you get to the customer's residence, ask if they want you to wear shoe covers or shoe booties. The reason you want to do this is because some people might not feel comfortable with dirty shoes coming in and out of the house stepping all over the floor. Some customers will tell you that they want you to take your shoes off while others will be a little shy about it.

This is why it's a good idea to ask when you get there to ensure that you're meeting the customer's needs. Sometimes, people will only care about you wearing shoe coverings in the new place that they're moving to. Every situation will be different, and you can avoid any sticky situation by buying some shoe covers ahead of time and asking if they need to be worn while inside the house. Small things like this can also lead to a better chance of getting a tip, so you might as well do it!

Squat Down Every Time

When it comes to moving, you're going to be picking things up off the floor a lot. A common tendency is for people to bend at the back to pick up items off the floor. You might do this regularly and not think anything of it.

Sure, plenty of people do this and it hasn't hurt them. However, you don't want to have this type of attitude towards your lifting technique. The reason for this is because all it takes is one wrong incident for your back to get injured.

Even if you're young and think you can take it, that bad technique will add more wear and tear to your body than necessary. If you're young right now, you'll be glad that you lifted properly when you get older. If you're already a bit older, then you really need to make sure your technique is on point.

I'm sure not lifting with your back is something you've heard before, but it's something we all need to be reminded of. There are going to be situations where it will be so simple and easy to just bend down and pick it up with your back, but don't fall for it.

Instead, squat down and pick the item up. This will help to disperse the pressure more evenly across your body as opposed to putting most of the strain in one area being your lower back.

Going Up Stairs

Going up and down stairs is a pain. It definitely isn't fun going up stairs backwards, but I think my best advice would be to take your time and move at the same pace. If two people are going up the stairs and the person on the bottom goes up faster than the person up top, it can make a bulky item get pushed into the person and cause them to get tripped up.

If both people go at the same pace, this won't be an issue. Also, the person at the bottom should raise the item up higher, if possible, as you go higher up the stairs. This will help to keep the item level for the person going backwards up the stairs.

The reason for this is because as the person going backwards goes up each step, it will increasingly create more of an angle away from parallel as you continue to climb if you keep the item at the same level. For example, let's say you and your partner are carrying a two-seater sofa up a flight of stairs. Your partner is going backwards up the stairs and you're at the bottom facing forward.

You both start carrying the couch on the ground to where the bottom of it is approximately at waist level for both of you. As you start to go up the stairs, the bottom of the couch will remain at waist level for you since you're at the bottom. However, it will slowly start to go to your partner's knees and even as low as their ankles depending on how steep the angle gets if you don't adjust where you're carrying the couch.

So as you start going up the stairs, move the couch from waist level, to chest level, to shoulder level if possible to make things easier for your partner when going up stairs. They're the person going backwards in this case, which is hard enough as it is anyways. You might as well do what you can to make things easier for them.

Make Sure You're Properly Covered

When moving, it's extremely important to be sure that every item you move is properly secured. For any item that isn't boxed up, put a pad over the item and then use shrink wrap to secure the item. You don't want to leave anything to chance.

A dolly could scratch an item. An item might be safely moved onto the truck, but it might be damaged on the truck depending on how things are packed. You still have to unload the truck and move the item into the new place, so it's a lot of moving that each item is undergoing. Using pads and shrink wrap will ensure that you mitigate the chances of damage to an item.

Along those same lines, this is why you'll want to use straps to ensure everything stays in place on the truck. Now imagine you strap a headboard to the wall of your truck, but you don't place a pad over it and secure it with shrink wrap. Now you're leaving yourself at risk for the headboard to get scratched, dirty, or possibly torn from metal clip inserts on your truck. It's best to use caution with every item that you handle.

Divide and Conquer

Let's assume it's you and one other person on a move. How should you go about getting the move done? You can really handle it a few different ways.

You both can take on one room at a time together, and start with bulky items that require two people to move. Once the big items are taken care of, you can split up and take smaller items individually until the room is cleared out and then move to the next room. You could split off right from the start and work in two separate rooms and then meet up to handle larger items.

Regardless, it's going to be better to split up when possible. If you have a third person on the crew, you have more ways you can approach things. Two people handle big items and the third person works on smaller items, or you could have the third person pack in the truck while the other two movers bring them items.

Packing a truck efficiently is a skill in and of itself. It's something you'll get better with as time goes on. Ideally, you'll want to pack in the truck with as little dead space as possible. Some general advice for how to do this is to stack bulky items on top of each other when possible.

For instance, let's say you're moving a dining table and two desks that together equal roughly the same surface area as the dining table. You can place the dining table right side up in the truck, and then you can stack the desks side-by-side upside down on top of the dining table. Now with this setup, you can still place smaller boxes on top of the desks and use straps to secure them in addition to placing smaller items underneath the dining table as well.

This way you end up with less dead space when compared to having the dining table right side up with boxes on it. Also be sure to place lighter items and boxes on top of heavier boxes. This is pretty basic advice, but you need to remember it when you're moving.

As time goes on, you're going to start to fatigue and/or things might be stacked in a way to where it's easy to stack something heavy on top of something light. This is something you don't want to do because it can definitely lead to a box getting punctured and items being damaged.

Chapter 6: Building Out Your Moving Team

Now it's time to talk about expansion. Maybe you're good with the company being yourself and someone else who helps you out. Maybe you want to grow your company as large as possible. In this chapter, I'm going to go over some things to help you out with expanding your business.

Really Consider What's Best for You

First and foremost, you need to stop and think about what you want to do. It may seem simple enough to want to grow and expand, but there are some benefits to staying small. You have less overhead costs, less problems to deal with, and you can still earn a great income.

If you want to expand, yes there's more you're going to have to deal with, but it will allow you to earn a lot more money. Also, you might get burnt out feeling like you're the one who has to handle everything. You have to market, handle scheduling and logistics, and actually execute every move.

Eventually, you might get to the point where you'll want to hire someone else to help take some of the load off of your plate. You might not though, and you might be able to handle things just fine as the main person.

Keep in mind, this isn't a decision you need to make as soon as you start your business. This is something you'll come to figure out as time goes on and you start to get busier.

Where Should You Go?

Let's assume you're at the point in your business where you're ready to make your first official hire. What position should you consider? Well, there are a lot of different roles that you can have as your company starts to get bigger.

There are sales positions, customer service, operations manager (to handle logistics, scheduling, managing movers, and any issues that the moving team may have during a move), team leads (aka lead mover who will be the first contact with the customer if any issues arise, handles getting remaining payment from customer at the end of the job, communicates with operations manager about potential issues, leads the way on how the move should be executed, and drives the box truck among other things), and team assistants (assist in helping with the move).

These are a lot of different positions that you could fill out. When you're smaller though, you simply won't be busy enough to justify one person for each role. For instance, you may have one person who handles customer service, scheduling, logistics, and manages the moving team or teams if it makes sense to do that based on where you are volume wise.

As I talked about earlier, I recommend that you start out with one other person that you use as a contractor on an as needed basis. This way you don't have to worry about consistently paying someone even if you're not steady with jobs. That money can instead go towards something such as marketing.

Let's say you start to get more consistent work and doing all of the business work along with being a part of every move is starting to be too much for you due to the newfound volume. What type of position should you hire? First, you really need to consider if this recent volume is consistent or more of a fluke.

If you're in peak season during the summer months, you may want to ride it out, if possible, and see how your volume is after peak season. You don't want to hire someone just for the work load to slow down and now you have an employee who doesn't have much to do, yet you still have to pay them. If your volume is still high even outside of the summer months, then that's a good indication that you can move forward with making a hire.

What role should you go for? Well, it's hard to say exactly because it will depend on just how high your current volume is. You might need to hire someone who handles a hybrid type of role.

They'll essentially split responsibilities with you. They'll go out on moves with you, but they'll also be able to share some of the customer service, scheduling and routing responsibilities. You can have them fully take on one or two of the operation roles such as customer inquiries and scheduling while you focus completely on marketing and handling any customer issues.

The other possibility is that everything is more so shared evenly between the two of you. If you're forming a partnership, then great; you already have someone who can share operation roles with you right from the start. If not, no worries; you're just going to have to find someone.

If your volume is higher, you could consider hiring a team lead and team assistant. This would allow you to completely remove yourself from actually moving customers and now you can focus solely on aspects of operating and growing the business. This still leaves the question as to how you can properly ensure that someone is fit for the job.

How Can You Hire a Good Fit for Your Company?

Making your first hire is a scary decision. You're committing to a person whom you consistently have to pay, and this person will be representing your company. This person will have a huge impact on your company one way or the other.

Make the right choice, and your business will climb to new heights easily and effortlessly. Make the wrong choice, and it can put you in a big hole quickly. So where should you look?

The first people you should consider are people you've worked with along the way as contractors. You worked with these people on moves, so you have a good understanding of their work ethic, attitude, if they show up on time, if they're a good mover, etc. If you worked with a solid contractor, then you should definitely consider offering a position to that person.

Working with someone out in the field is a much better way to gauge how they'll be as an employee compared to an interview. This person may not have any experience with an operation type of role, and that's completely fine. You can train them on those aspects if you want to hire a position for operating the business.

The fact that they have experience in the field will help them with running the business. If you don't have any reliable contractors that you feel comfortable moving forward with, where should you turn to next? Start looking at people you already know. Maybe you've worked for a moving company previously or had a similar type of job.

Hit up your previous coworkers, and see if they're interested in applying for your new role. Even if you haven't worked directly in the moving field, you might know people who have, so contact them and see. It doesn't hurt to try.

If you don't know of any good candidates from people you already know, then it's going to be time to enlist some outside help. You can do this by using a job recruiting website and posting a job ad. This will help to create a lot of candidates for your job.

Yes, you'll have to pay to post a job ad, but it will be well worth it. Trying to source your own candidates is a job in and of itself. Keep in mind that you still have to run your business. It's far easier to pay and have another company bring candidates to you.

What to Look for When Someone Applies to Your Job

You're going to receive a lot of different people applying to your job to the point where it can get overwhelming. So what are some things you should look out for when it comes to hiring? The first thing you want to look at is job experience.

What kinds of jobs has this person worked previously? If you're hiring for an operations type of role, previous experience in the moving field is going to be the best case. They'll have a keen understanding of issues that can happen and how to solve them.

If they've worked in operations in a different field, that's not necessarily a bad thing. They can still be a very good worker, but they'll need to get up to speed on how things work in the moving world. If you're hiring a mover, you'll definitely want them to have relevant work experience.

Moving consistently as a job is strenuous, and it certainly isn't for everyone. People who haven't worked as a mover before typically can't grasp just how strenuous the job can be at times. They might not last long at the job, but you can't assume that.

If you hire someone who has been a mover before, that person knows exactly the kind of work the job is going to entail. This isn't to say you need to immediately disregard candidates that don't have relevant work experience. It's more so to say that people with relevant work experience should jump towards the top of your list if everything else checks out.

After you look at their previous jobs, you also need to consider how long they've been at their previous jobs. For example, someone might have had three different jobs in the past year. If you hire this person, what are the chances that they leave you within 3-4 months?

It's a very real possibility because this person appears to be a job hopper, or maybe they're a bad worker and have been let go from multiple jobs. You want to hire a candidate who has good job stability. Ideally, someone would have been at a previous job for at least a year.

The other thing you want to look for is a job gap. This isn't necessarily a bad thing, as life can be unpredictable and anything can happen. There could be a very valid reason as to why someone wasn't able to work.

You'll just want to make sure you ask them about their job gap if the person is worthy for an interview. If they have a year-long job gap and tell you that it was just hard for them to find a job, then you should be skeptical. You don't know how many jobs the person applied to every day, but the story seems fishy.

That's a big job gap and for all you know it could've been due to a lack of effort. If you come across someone that you like, here are some questions and prompts you can bring up during the interview:

-Tell me a little bit about yourself.

-What is your biggest strength?

-What is your biggest weakness?

-If the candidate doesn't have direct experience working in the moving industry: How will your previous role at blank company help you with this job?

-If the candidate is strictly an operations type of role: Would you be willing to help out on moves, if necessary? (This way you'll have someone who can cover if someone on the moving team calls in sick or for various other reasons.)

-If a candidate is applying for team lead or team assistant without previous related work experience: This is a heavy physical labor job. Tell me how you're capable of handling a physical load for 8 hours a day.

-How would your previous coworkers describe you?

-For team leads and operation manager type roles: What is your leadership style? (You'll want to hire someone who has a similar type of style as you. You don't want to bring on someone who demands orders all of the time if you're more of a lead by example type of person. It will make it harder for you to get on the same page with the candidate if you do hire them.)

-Finish off the interview by asking if the candidate has any questions for you. If they don't, this could be a sign that they don't care or they simply haven't thought about it and they aren't prepared. It's a good sign if they ask one or two well thought out questions to you.

If the interview goes well, all is not done. You'll want to make sure that you complete a background check on the person before you hire them. You never know what could be a part of someone's past, and if there is something concerning, there's a low chance they're going to bring it up to you.

Some people will though, if they suspect that a background check is coming. Either way, you have to run a background check simply because you just never know. You might be hiring for a team lead position, and someone unfortunately might have a history with DUIs, but you wouldn't know unless you run a background check.

You also want to call one or two references as well before making a hire. If a candidate is unable to provide any references, this could be a red flag. The candidate might not want you talking to previous employers because they know they aren't going to receive high praise.

If you call the references and hear positive feedback about the person, then that's a great sign. Hearing good words from a previous employer is a good indication of how this person will work. If the interview goes well, they pass the background check, pass a drug test (which could be a requirement for them to be able to be put on your insurance as a driver), and have good references, then you've got yourself a good candidate!

Conclusion

Starting a moving company is far from easy. It takes a lot of effort and money just to get things going. The work itself can also be hard labor at times.

Even with that being the case, the money you can make is well worth the effort. Maybe you're not someone who wants to sit at a desk all day. You want to be out and about on the road and move your body.

I totally get that. Luckily, with this business, you get the chance to do that each and every day. Maybe you want to eventually hire a team and take on more of an operations role or take a back seat completely.

Either way is totally fine, and the good news is that it's up to you to decide how you want to go about things. This is your business, and no one else can tell you how to run things.

I hope this book was a helpful guide for you in your business journey. Remember, it's not always going to be easy, but it's going to be worth it, so hang in there!